Triangle

A triangle has three sides.
Can you find the missing stickers?

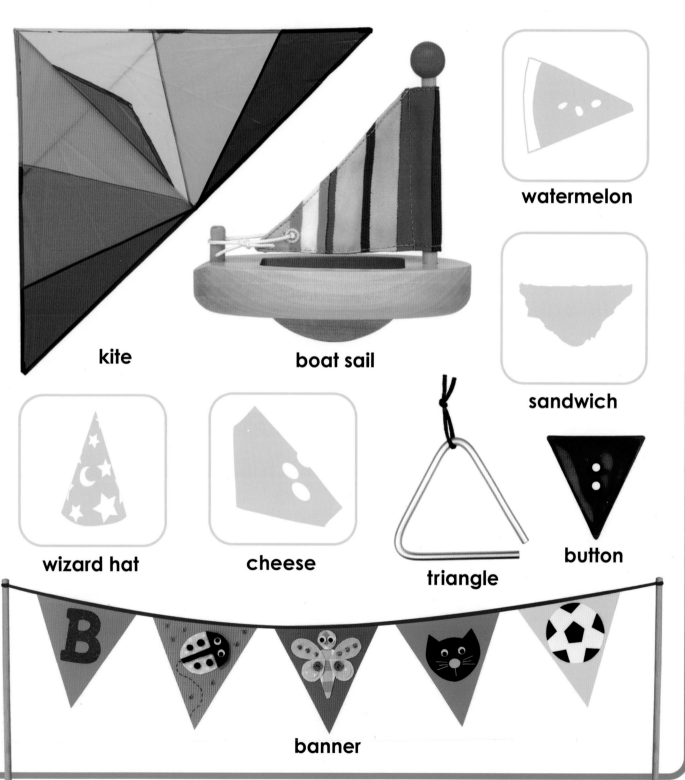

kite

boat sail

watermelon

sandwich

wizard hat

cheese

triangle

button

banner

1

Square

A square has four equal sides.
Can you find the missing stickers?

cushion

dice

cracker

picture frames

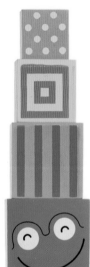

gift

button

toast

blocks

Circle

A circle has no sides.
Can you find the missing stickers?

orange slice

clock

beads

roll of tape

button

marbles

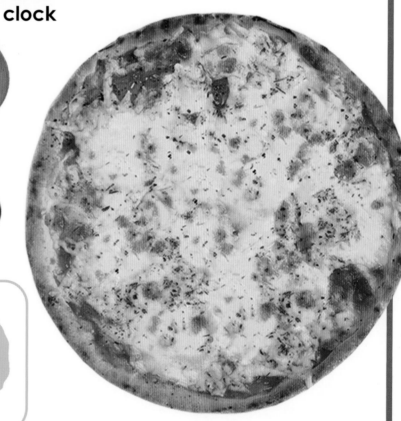

pizza

wheel

cucumber slice

Oval

An oval is a round, flattened shape. Can you find the missing stickers?

bar of soap

bread roll

avocado

candy

football

ladybug

Easter egg

egg

balloon

Rectangle

A rectangle has two long sides and two short sides. Can you find the missing stickers?

picture frame

dominoes

gemstone

ruler

window

treasure chest

envelope

puzzle

Star

A star has many points.
Can you find the missing stickers?

pencil sharpener

bath toy

jewel

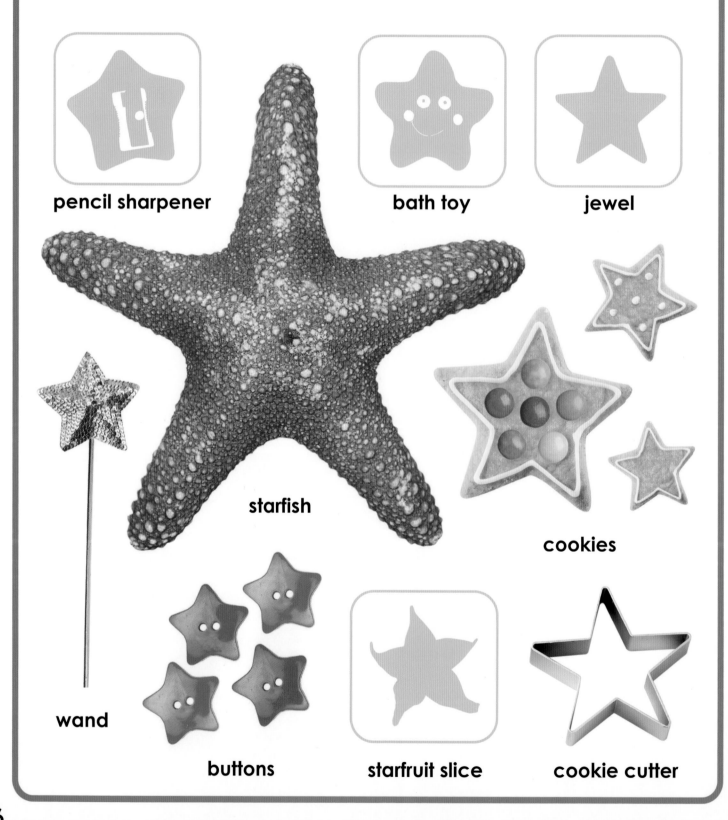

starfish

cookies

wand

buttons

starfruit slice

cookie cutter

6

Heart

A heart has curves and a point.
Can you find the missing stickers?

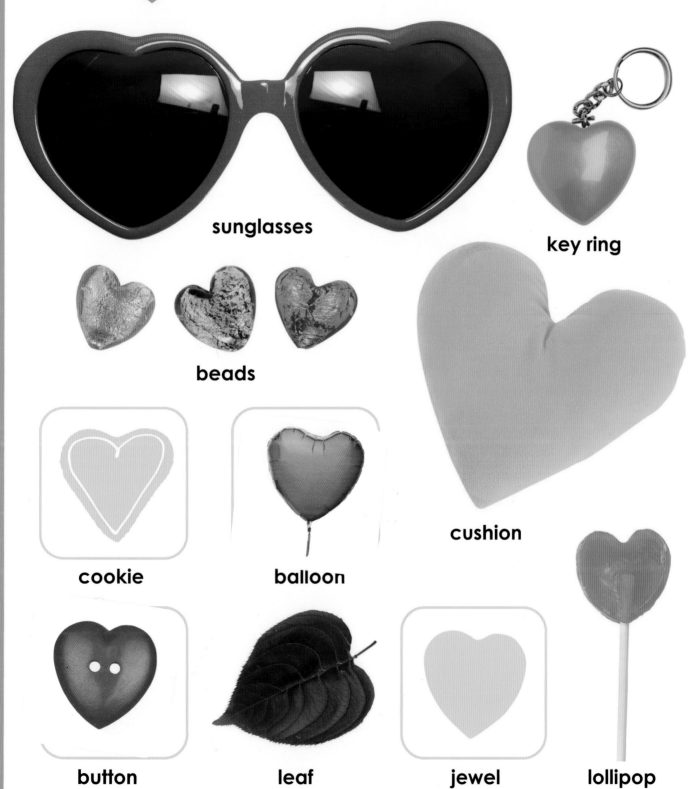

sunglasses

key ring

beads

cushion

cookie

balloon

button

leaf

jewel

lollipop

Patterns

Can you find the missing
stickers to complete the shape patterns?

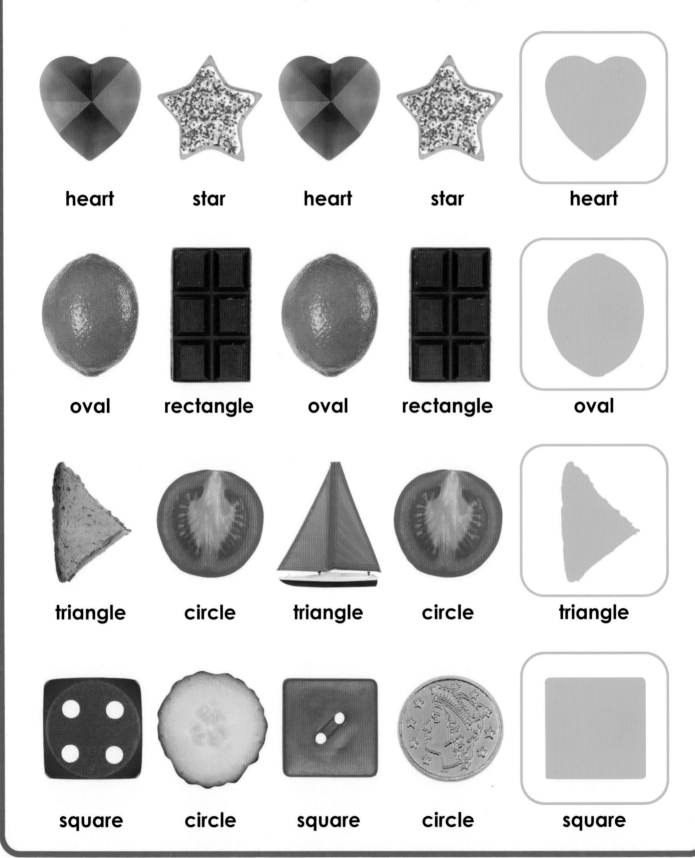

heart	star	heart	star	heart
oval	rectangle	oval	rectangle	oval
triangle	circle	triangle	circle	triangle
square	circle	square	circle	square

8

Sorting

Can you find the stickers to sort the shapes?

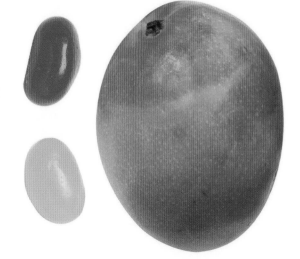

Oval

Rectangle

9

Shapes

Choose more stickers for each shape.

 ## Triangle

 ## Oval

 ## Square

Shapes

Choose more stickers for each shape.

 **Circle**

 **Rectangle**

 **Star**

Heart

Shape match

Put the shaped objects onto the matching shapes.

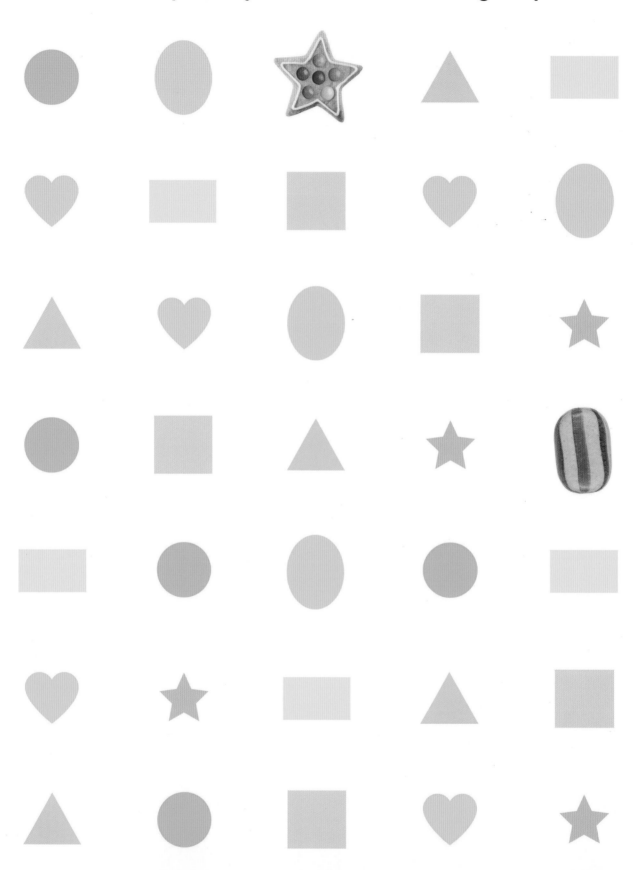

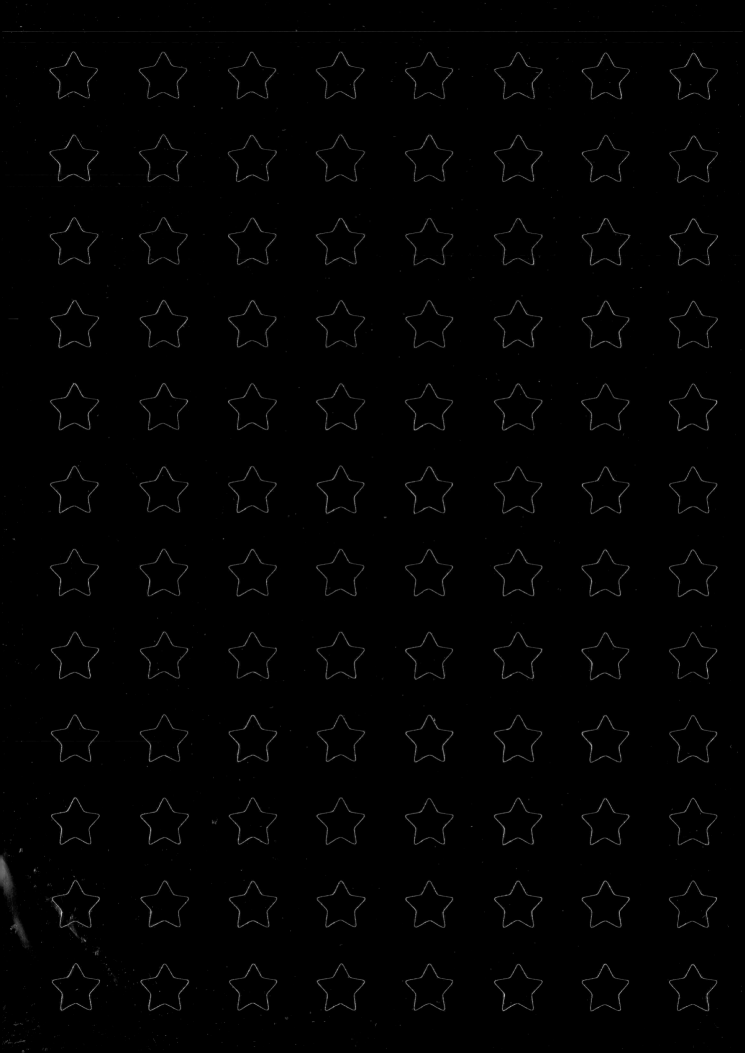

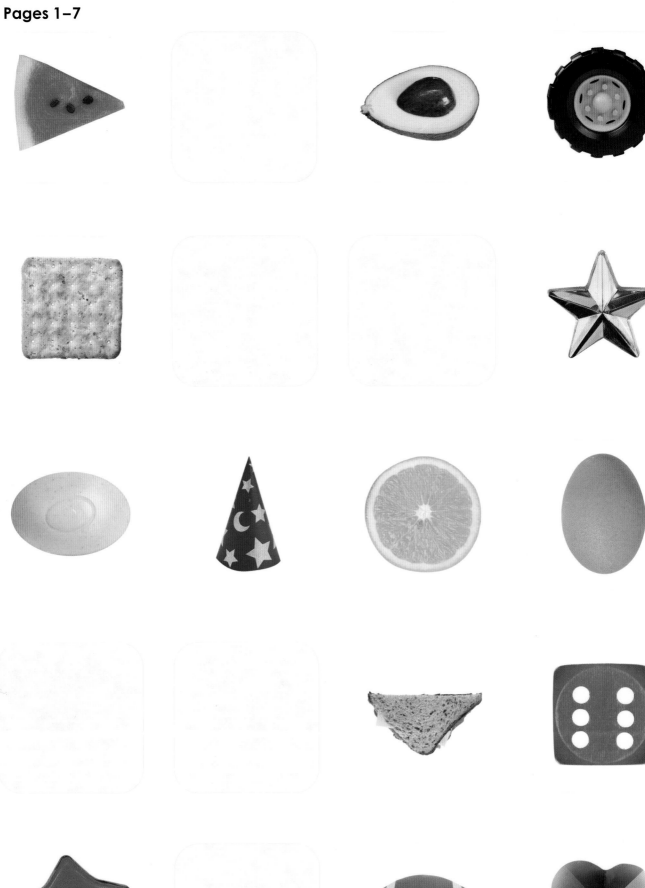

 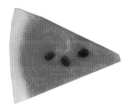  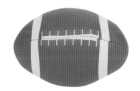